BEARINGS

JOHN EGBERT

ISBN: 979-8-218-41261-6

Library of Congress Control Number: 2024907704

Illustrations by Laurie Egbert
Book Design by Jill Flores

First printing edition 2024

For
Laurie, Grace, Lucia

Acknowledgments

After teaching history and natural history in New Mexico, I reached out to improve my creative writing process. I discovered Priscilla Long's Taos Writer's Workshop class on sentences and paragraphs. I joined Richard Tillinghast's poetry workshop at the Bear River Writers in Michigan. Kevin Murphy and Linda Conroy of Bellingham have been inspirational. These gifted writers are also gifted teachers.

In New Mexico, through Priscilla, the late Seattle poet Judith Roche critiqued my poems over the phone. I began to listen to what worked well, and what needed changing. After moving to Bellingham in 2018, Priscilla introduced me to Bethany Reid of Edmonds. Bethany, a retired English professor and published poet, met with me over Zoom for two years: closely reading, questioning, suggesting, yet always supporting my ownership and final decisions on language.

My wife, Laurie, created the cover painting and my daughter Grace prepared it for the cover. My daughter, Lucia, has supported me in infinite ways since we moved from New Mexico to Bellingham in 2017.

Thank you to layout and cover designer Jill Flores. Thank you to Village Books Publishing for guiding me through the publishing process.

Contents

Introduction

Reading forward, you will experience gardens, wildlife, deserts, forests, lakes and rivers, various human and animal characters, including myself, a bit of political innuendo, and linguistic exploration. The intent of the book is to offer a wide range of people and places to be seen and felt in new ways. I do throw curves, perhaps keeping you off balance with so much variety in each of this volume's twelve poem clusters.

I have been a rambler since childhood. After a career in teaching history and natural history, I keep traveling and talking to people. A trip may be in my neighborhood to spy on bumblebees deep into hollyhocks, or to a lake or river to fish where I may fish alone or meet other fishermen. I could be gardening in Bellingham, teaching in Albuquerque, hiking with friends on New Mexico's Gila River, or taking a fishing break to bird watch in Patagonia.

I love wandering in New Mexico's desert in search of spring wildflowers or during the monsoon for spadefoot toads. I've discovered that Stellar's Jays warble like mockingbirds on the edge of the Pacific temperate rainforest. In New Mexico's mountains, they may whistle, but usually they scold, seem grittier, and less adaptable to human settlement. The tropical rainforest has become another source of wonder; remarkable to be in a place where native species and a full-blown green aesthetic overwhelm a naturalist acclimated to dry, brown, grassy, wide-open spaces. New Mexico and Ecuador feel like two different planets. Sit quietly on a log in the Pacific Northwest rainforest or Ecuador, or propped up on boulder in the desert and you begin to feel the underpinnings of life.

My contention is that travel informs, builds a reservoir of perspectives on life regardless of language or place. Experiencing differences breeds tolerance and love of fellow creatures and humanity. I hope this feeling is conveyed, that poems will exact empathy and breed a desire to expand your own perspectives. Travel need not be exotic.

If I had explored New Mexico beyond my 45 years there, I'd be able to offer more. Changing venues has, I believe, kept me star struck, a feeling I like, but don't depend on. My home garden and people I meet where I live, or old friends, keep changing. Paying attention is its own trip.

Reading my own work has helped deepen my past, and I hope, be open to more people and nature's wild and surprising complexity. I have tried to focus so you can join me in these moments. Sometimes analytical, maybe sentimental, often romantic, searching for beauty, and finding it.

As for me, I'm outgoing, distractible, yet able to hyper-focus. I find it easy to engage with people. I like people and my feelings seem to convey that I can be trusted. I am not a whisperer or aggressive, but I think approachable and as I hope this text proves, caring enough to invest in others.

Mood of mind and moment trigger poems: people and nature create surprises that draw me in. A line, a stanza, a rhythm develops. Some blossom. Some fade. Either way, love of the moment begs questions and refrains. I can tie knots or bows. I wish each reader well in their discoveries herein and perhaps challenged to dig more thoroughly into your place and people, and reach out to those near or far.

Screech Owl

Above our porch,
a screech owl posed
on a dead tree:
hushed,
nodded,
blinked,
questioned little me.
I'd heard it hoot
from the kitchen
before I felt its
yellow eyes
slit through mine.

— Childhood home in Glendale, Ohio, circa 1953

Androsace

Dainty desert primrose,
Pleistocene whim,
shooting star sponged from snow,
pops like corn in granitic scree,
bows to ancestral seed
ridden up and down the slope
with gusts and flakes,
finds a crack to sprout.

Revere the gray fox
that fertilize your pink rosettes,
ponderosas that mulch your bed.
Wonder about pioneers who slashed and burned,
who threw kitchen tables overboard.
Be happy you have all you need
when we complain of drought
below our reservoir and fear of fire.
Be happy you're not the man who
left his blue tent sagging
over your patch of white flowers
to search for food in town.

Some of us would be better rooted here
like *Androsace*,
our tongues sipping from the soil,
no need to gallivant about the earth.

Androsace septentrionalis,
a native primrose common to the
Sangre de Cristo Mountains,
6,500 to 12,00 feet elevation.

Bellingham Flowers

The block is long, uphill.
I sniff from flower to flower,
catch my breath
on morning glories.

If my grandson stood beside me,
I'd stick my nose into a round, blue blossom,
inhale deeply so pleats would stick.

Over the stone wall,
blackberries push their canes,
poke ferocity
through English ivy,
stealing heather's sun.

A pink phlox raceme
slips between brambles, vines, vanilla,
peonies shedding petals,
smashed clam shells on the street.

Yellow, red, and pink
hollyhocks spiral up,
sprout from the ash of the old hotel.

I imagine hydrangeas in the lobby.
A silver vase of callas funnel above the hearth.
Bridesmaids, gardenia-scented,
swarm the bride like honeybees.

Thinking of Trees

Below the oaks, above the pond,
I overheard a fellow telling his friend
he knew a white oak from a red.
"The leaf," he chastened,
taking off his glasses.
His friend wearing a Red Sox hat,
didn't seem to care.

"It's the measure of its waist
which differentiates the two,"
one leaf shapely and divine,
the other not so thick,
a river to a stream of sorts.

He held up two leaves,
spun them in one hand,
ran his finger up and down,
the white oak a roller coaster
braking around the bristly red.

I looked the other way
knowing sometimes
I tell people more than they want to know.

I grew up with Ohio oaks,
whites with soft, rounded fingers,
reds with scalloped troughs, spiny teeth.
And maples: sugar maple leaves
with broad palms like sycamores,
smaller palmate Norway's,
a deep cut silver that
shaded my bedroom window.

Sixty years later,
I still feel my hands gripping
a Norway maple limb,
knuckling to the sky,
fingers, thumbs
tight into the bark.
My right foot
digs into a knot,
my left scrambles for a notch.
Nearing the tippy top,
I feel the leader bend,
the pull of land,
that dwarfs what I understand.

— *Walden Pond, Massachusetts, October 31, 2010*

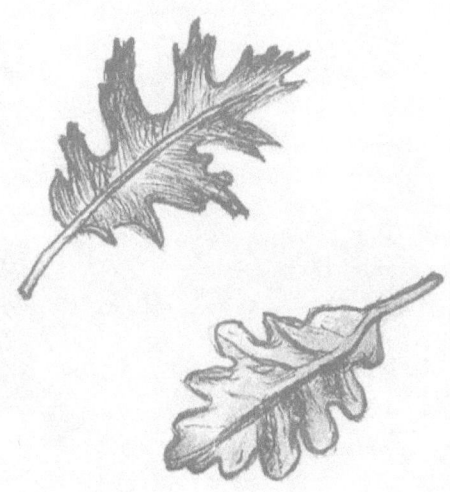

Answer Mark

I love a question mark,
a shepherd's staff
to hook a fox
to save a lamb,
drive half way round the rotary
when we forget directions.

In our shorthand world,
why is there no answer mark
to show what we feel is true?

I suggest a circle with a star,
asterisk inside an O,
like spokes,
no need for reins or ropes,
a steel-rimmed wagon wheel to cross the prairie,
a propeller to cross the sea.

Jemez Heart

I sit on your river rock,
feel your boombox beat.

A robin stands on the bank,
tilts its head, flies up,
perches in an alder.
A dipper bobs, dives,
cold water to cleanse a soul.

I'm here to stop scolding the world,
turn my ear to tumbling water,
current rumbling through my heart.

— *Jemez Mountains, New Mexico, April 18, 2008*

Your Self

How wonderful to draw out your geometry:
triangles, corners,
circles, bends and breaches,
quadrangles, wavy lines and tangents.
Show your colors blue and green,
a budding leaf upon its stem,
a crest that rides the waves,
a cloud you know will rain,
or clear, when clouds foretell the sun.

The Southern Border

Why haven't we cut these swales of grass
to feed our cows, to make our cheese?
Let it waste away under the dirigible's eye?

Washington, who are you to guide
the farmer and the rancher
who need Mexicans to pick our apples,
to milk our cows, to brand our bulls?
Mexicans who need us to supply their families here and there.

Dare we ask the sparrows and the Sparrow Hawk?
What shall they advise who know no bounds?

— *Patagonia, Arizona, February 20, 2015*

Note:
U.S. unmanned dirigibles hang above the border using radar and other
sensors to detect people.

To A Mourning Cloak Butterfly

I am turning alkaline soil
to dig in pink *Agastache*,
my favorite licorice mint
for hummingbirds and butterflies.
I'm mixing gravel
so roots can breathe.

My breath flutters
with a mourning cloak
basking on the sunny river rock:
flat black, blue-eyed border, yellow fringe,
spread thin as wind paints spring.

— *Albuquerque, New Mexico, April 5, 2008*

Note:
Agastache cana Hummingbird mint

Meadowlark

A band of yellow-breasted meadowlarks
gathers with Gretchen's goats.
I watch birds pluck grasshoppers off frosted leaves,
strut between gray tomato vines,
raise their heads and freeze.
Several meadowlarks erupt in sharp-winged flight,
drop like ducks into the puddled pasture with a mule.

I was once a plain, white bird
before I heard a meadowlark singing from a yucca stalk,
a flute to carry me through life.
I've wandered the open earth,
thirsted for its space:
rim-rocked mountains, turgid rivers, bristling seas;
napped under oaks where quail have tickled me;
cast a willow wand
to childhood dreams;
blown forty years ago across the continent,
a droplet in the desert.

I've watched friends become
hawks, sparrows,
crows, parrots and parakeets,
bellbirds that chime from treetops,
wrens that whine or whistle from ferny stumps,
a carillon of finches that rally to the feeder.

I love meadowlarks' garden haunts,
the upland swales with grassy clumps.
Yet, I could never be a meadowlark
tucked into the hayfield's edge,
glean seeds and beetles,
rely on my brown back for camouflage,
wary of the fox.
I'm more the swift who cruises cliffs,
a harrier hovering over hummocks,
a Short-eared Owl in Labrador.

— *Gila, New Mexico, November, 2015*

On the Banks of Rito Hondo

Two men sat on the bank of Rito Hondo,
a lake whose chill exceeded the howls of coyotes
baying high on the edge of aspens,
where breezes turned to gusts
to shut down idle chatter,
sent the men fishing leeward,
casting elsewhere to the edge of moss,
where suspicions lay for brook trout
nosing about for snails, leeches, green midge larvae.

The fishermen hunched in their lawn chairs,
hoped that Power Bait
combined the essence of this natural mess;
just yesterday proved their point,
hit on food fish dream of.

For myself, finning on the water,
and confident in my Peacock Lady fly
of Arizona fame,
I took the drift in stride,
cast through wind with
a small mess of my own,
a few feathers wrapped about a hook.

My tack around the point
took me before the older men
who strung up bobbers easily as tying shoes,
who lay in wait of judgment of themselves or me
about our abilities that day,
who told me they had fished the lake for twenty years,
same side, same bank, same point
cut down from spruce edges,
marmot whistles, elk trails.

In a breeze we talked.
With a squall we huddled
like ruddy ducks,
our heads hidden under canvas caps,
casting, retrieving
smooth as spinning wheels,
waiting, wondering
since fish were never true.

Notes:
Rito Hondo Lake lies at 10,250' elevation below Slumgullion Pass,
San Juan Mountains, Colorado.

Power Bait is made from PVC, a scented polyvinyl chloride.

Crows

As a boy playing in cornfields
in my Ohio village,
I learned crow cries and calls.
My friend Chris, who raised a baby crow from the nest,
taught me crows were smarter
than all the other birds whose nests they rob,
cagey loud, gunsmoke black,
ventriloquial pets, farmers' pests.

Crows harassed me and friends
when we rolled corn husks and smoked the silk.

I've seen crows fall dead from the sky.
I've tied their feathers into fishing flies.

In Bellingham,
they dive on us like kamikazes,
snip our hair if we approach their nest
set deep in the green holly outside our porch.
Sentries caw at us from the school parapet,
the chimney on the yellow house next door,
or threaten us eating lunch.
I beg for peace when their babies fledge,
but they swoop on us like hornets
as if we are to blame for the world's ills,
as if we think crows could understand
we have no intention of eating crow.

— *Bellingham, Washington, June, 2016*

Arroyo Cairns

I walk this arroyo cut down
below stuccoed walls
baring roots of junipers and pines.
I love this slice of nature pie,
sluice of feldspar grays and pinks,
green epidote and white quartz,
a bull snake skin curling through
camel humps of sand,
a Scrub Jay begging me to disappear.

You, the artist arrive
like some ancient Native initiate,
some finger-painting kindergarten kid,
come to stack stones,
as if to sanctify reparations for all of us
who have carved or cast this earth.

August's flood sweeps away
rabbit pellets, piñon hulls,
a towhee's white tail feather.
Footprints vanish.
Cairns survive.

— *Santa Fe, New Mexico, 2015*

William Enderes' Mandolin

When Aunt Daisy invited me
to search her garage,
I discovered a melon mandolin
that lay for years under the sagging roof.

Her brother Will, a doctor,
who died at 23,
left behind the mountaineer
in a green canvas-covered steamer trunk.

The mandolin slept with white Victorian petticoats,
a powderhorn, a Franco-Prussian bayonet.
Surviving love and war,
she'd settled in with Daddy Longlegs,
Uncle Bob's black shoes and suits,
an American flag with 48 stars.

I took her home, hung her up with fishing line
on my bedroom wall with a bamboo pole.

She's stayed with me in apartments,
houses, a cowboy shack I used to own.
I carved her a tuning peg from an elk antler,
paid a luthier to glue and strap her back together.
I'll have to find a picker,
wish it were Bill Monroe.

— *Hamilton, Ohio and New Mexico*

19

Belmullet Bay

You forget that the fruits belong to all
and that the land belongs to no one.
— Jean-Jacques Rousseau

I tramp through puddles to the wild Atlantic edge,
scatter curlews from their mossy beds.
Oystercatchers poke into tidal flats.
Gulls chase each other for rotten crabs.
A skylark warbles in the wind.
A Friesian cow nurses spotted calves,
its black bull shackled with ring and chain.

I admire a solitary, pastured cob,
15 hands, pied like wagtails of her pasture,
silky-tailed, shaggy-maned.
I stroke her muzzle,
hand her grass.

A silver car bumps down the muddy path.
John, the horse's owner,
comes to haul food and water to young Bess.
We shake hands.
"You're American, I guess?"

John, recent foreman of a peat power plant,
has built a seaside home,
reclaims his childhood on his farm,
raises Bess to pull his cart,
fills her water bucket,
her basket full of hay,
tips his hat and drives away.

I'd like to return to the country, too,
I, without a Gaelic brogue,
whose ears turn green for fiddle, fife,
who envies those who live near sea.

How would I steer my course
except wade for salmon in the spring?

I'd meet village people
in the bakeries and the pubs,
walk the beach admiring dulse and kelp,
talk to John about Irish breeds,
but never buy a horse.

I'd confess myself a foreigner,
a migrant shorebird Ruff.

— *Belmullet Bay, Ireland, April, 2017*

Apricots

Frost decides if apricots will set,
filling out as children do,
green to gold,
sweetening up like honey.

I cheer our tree slurping slush all winter,
reinventing itself for another year
like we do in Santa Fe
scratching out new lives amongst the piñon,
our easels set up under cottonwoods
above May's rushing river.

Dare we peek at March's budding tree this morning?
Are petals popping?
Is pollen whispering with the buzz of bees?

Will we be filling jars in June?
Will we drip jam on buttered toast?

Rock House Sparrows

In a one room cabin
sunk into Guerrero canyon's slope,
I breathe the burnt-wood smell of creosote,
old railroad ties salvaged from the copper mine.
I slip into my sleeping bag,
and prop a pillow behind my head.
Massive ceiling joists stare down on me
that once held up the Gila River bridge.

Below the garden, the windmill aches,
its sucker rod asleep.
From the bamboo thicket,
I hear sparrows chatter
half-witted with the stars,
as if the flock might stir the universe.
Pitch black inside the rock house,
I shuffle to the cabin door
to shush the birds so I can doze.
Night passes.
I wake with crickets
before shade or shadow.
The thrasher warbles, whistles,
calling up the sun.

— *Gila, New Mexico, March 18, 2014*

Note:
Wintering White-crowned Sparrows and a resident Curve-billed Thrasher.

Confoundation

Does poetry know
one planet from another,
sun from moon,
Mars from Earth,
you from me,
calculus or geometry?

I asked Shakespeare the other day
if he were she, or she was he.
I asked leopard if its spots are real,
egg if yolk is yellow,
sky if I'm seeing sun,
what I hope are not its final rays.

I asked Galileo if he
believed in Darwin,
said he'd never met the man.
I asked Jesus if he believed in Brutus,
said he'd never met the man.
I asked my father if he knew my mother,
said he might remember her.
She said the same of him.
Shall I ask my children who I am?

Two Girls Playing in the Woods

I haven't found anything kinder
than two girls playing in the woods,
cross-legged on a rock banging sticks in time
like tree frogs rapping out evening songs.

Why can't I shrink to three feet tall,
crouch to find more mushrooms,
be the hide of seek,
lay hidden behind blue spruce
curling fingers through the moss?

I want to shatter bones
ossified between my ears,
be that rubber kid again,
star-saddled on the moon.

— *Sangre de Cristos above Santa Fe, New Mexico, July 28, 2015*

Wig

Wig leaned over his handlebars,
pumped his pedals by our house like burly briar,
scythe slung over his back,
crusty fedora hat.

One morning,
we crossed paths on my way to baseball
on a rise where two people usually say hello.
Aged ten, I dared say "Hi."

Peeking up through his muffy beard,
Wig grumbled,
"You better watch out, buddy."
I'd evaded Butch Henderson's curveball,
had my share of friendly fights with friends.
That day, I faced a troll.

In the fall, I dared speak again
to Wig on Gunny Hill.
He bragged of younger days,
a soldier in the war with Spain,
a last survivor, he proclaimed,
of a great American cause.

I watched Wig slay fields of weeds
along Coral Avenue,
slice down thistle,
crowns off Queen Anne's Lace.
Wig lived nowhere,
just passed through one yard to the next,
swept his scythe,
kept time in trim.

— *Glendale, Ohio, 1955*

Melon

Mustard days pass to summer.
Late winter clouds pucker
like old men sucking lemon drops.

Like broth,
earth waits for the potato.
Melon wades towards
the sun.

— *Albuquerque, New Mexico, 2008*

Tunkwa Lake Exchange

The man in the blue jacket and blue jeans
has driven south from Dawson Creek
to catch a fish for his mother.
He's been fishing with a spinning rod,
dunking worms, had no bites.

Above the bank at Tunkwa Lake,
he gives me an orange pumpkin-headed fly.
I cast it, let it sink where I'd observed a trout.

A rainbow inhales the imitation,
jumps, tugs and jerks.
I play the fish, reel hard,
turn its head to shore.
He hands me his net.
I scoop the flopping fish.
I offer it to him.

He drops his eyes, turns away,
pushes his canoe from shore into the bay.

I watch him cast
towards the oozing sun.
I focus on his rod,
and hope to see it bend.

— *British Columbia, 2020*

Pipistrelle

Sitting on a crabapple stump at dusk,
I admire a pipistrelle,
a tiny bat, neither light nor shadow,
flicking, flickering in black and white,
electrons splitting time and space.

When I was young,
I nearly failed chemistry unable to imagine
a universe built on charges,
particles assigned to what I used to think
was life and death,
food and drink,
rocks and sand,
something I could understand.

As a boy, I watched
bats circle the silver maple
outside my unscreened bedroom window.
One flew inside,
crisscrossed in figure eights,
frightened me.
I squirm recalling how
I swatted the bat with a tennis racket,
picked it off the floor by its broken wing.

— *Glendale, Ohio, 1957*
— *Bellingham,*
Washington, 2021

Mother Tongue

Ticklish words that make us laugh,
dangle ambiguity
when questions beg
a, b, c, d,
or none of the above.
A stroke of pen,
an X to nix,
script for war,
roots for texts
dug from Ganges, Tiber, Spix,
sounds that spit, spam, spell,
breathe a song
with trebles, clefts,
letters treading on each other's tails.

River Fishing

Like a beaver,
I shuffle to the water,
rise up like a salmon-searching bear.
I'm no otter,
more a caterpillar bobbing for a leaf,
no diving dipper, water rolling off my back.
If I were a mallard,
dabbling in the eddy,
I'd be fine, water striders at my side.

I've come to fish for river trout,
karma thick or thin,
to probe the riffles,
tap cobbles with my wading staff,
feel rubble rook by knight,
bend my knees, wed my heels,
dodge deep holes, slippery rocks,
plug each foot cork to cask.

I swing the rod, raise the line,
sew a seam to reach the alder sweeper,
lay down the fly like a fallen feather.

Blackberries

I push into the brambles,
stretch my rocking ribs,
turtle-necked, tip-toed,
to grapple the ripest fruit,
fat juicy blackberries with fading sheen.
I pry, weave, wiggle my hands
between, over, under thorny canes,
snag my sleeves.
My cotton shirt becomes a rag.

Purple fingers tell me I'm alive.
I'll grow an inch,
fumble fruit.
I'm good at spilling love.

— Bellingham, Washington, August, 2021

Walking in Mount Auburn Cemetery

A cemetery is no place for death.
Thousands of souls vanished.
Tons of polished granite
chipped with God's sledge, the Jesus chisel.

A red sandstone grotto entombs Henry Cabot Lodge.
Longfellow's grave is long and hard embraced by green grass.
For Winslow Homer, scattered mussel shells lay above his head.
Will the painter's hand put them back together, jib to mast?

Looking up into sugar maples,
I'm thrown by catbird rants
balanced with cardinal whistles,
a vireo's tweedledee-tweedledum.

At my feet, white bells of lily of the valley
shrivel in morning heat,
their chimes ringing for me since childhood.
I stop and read Mary Baker Eddy's marble epitaph,
"Science is an emanation of divine mind."
I can hear Steven Jay Gould's retort,
"The mind is fully explicable by science."

Spider silk threads,
backlit in sunshine, swirl
like errant balloons from a birthday party.
I jive with dashing souls fed with worms
strumming for robins.
An inchworm dangles in my face.
From where?
Heaven?

— *Cambridge, Massachusetts, May, 2012*

Wenatchee Orchard Wedding

The American president is calling for a
round-up of migrant workers.
— news item, April, 2017

On our Seattle flight,
a woman doctor from Gallup
where she works with the Indian Health Service,
tells me she's on her way
to a farm worker wedding:

a Mexican woman
and Chinese-Peruvian man
struggle to find a preacher;
the best man left for Mexico;
tamales will be talking,
mariachis need a double bass.

Green spires push
through manure
at atmospheric speed.
Who will pick asparagus?

Funnel Weaver at Sand Ranch

Tickling your tablecloth,
the silken sheet you've laid,
your invitation for visitors to dance,
to tap their toes on your woven mesh
just long enough for you to raze the party.

I've seen folks like you
behind their computer screens or in the halls,
their demeanor, like your funnel,
pricked by the slightest twitch,
ready to pounce.

I'm that way myself at times,
although rarely ready to bite the mouth that's feeds.

"Spider, I'm the one who grabbed a stick,
scraped your web from a bowl of sand
under the crouching yucca,
choosing to let the cricket live.
You can weave another trap,
do your business as I do mine."

— *Mescalero Sands, New Mexico, September, 2006*

The Cat in the At

Appreciation for Dr. Seuss, *The Cat in the Hat*, 1957,
and John Keats, *Ode On A Grecian Urn*, 1819

The *Cat in the Hat*,
or was it the *Cat in the At*,
without bat, dat, eat or fat?

Eat?
Good eats as in
beets,
or fats,
feats,
dare I ask Keats?

I am no foster child of silence
in the vat with the cat,
pickled beets or sticky sweets
sprinkled with cinnamon
of dear sticky bun.
Don't dare go there.
Go back to at
as in "Where are you at
my dear cat?"

I think I'm on to a syllogism prism,
the grammar hammer,
to be right for English
despite its chasms,
truth through proper dopper,
when at beats me up
playing in that musty urn,
that silly hat.

To Catch a Fish

I hope the Rio Grande
will be full of fish for
Pueblo kids,
soon-to-be fisher boys and girls
who we teach to cast
on the Indian School court.

Norman shows them how to
push four rod pieces together:
top to bottom, thin to thick.
Slip the reel into the notch,
screw it down.
Run slick green fly line
through silver ferrules
of a gray graphite fishing pole.

Kids wing backcasts
like hook shots.
Line sails above their heads,
a forward snap of Velcro fly
grabs the toy trout's bullseye.

A woman in a car
rolls down her window,
points at all of us and laughs,
"All they need is a string,
a safety pin and a worm."

— *Santa Fe Indian School, New Mexico, April 11, 2016*

Note:
Norman Maktima is a Pueblo fishing guide, artist, and teacher.

Vermont May

Searching for morels,
I trudge in tractor ruts
filled with mud and apple petals.
Barefoot in boots,
I parse a poem's lips:
a silver leaf floating
on the bucket's brim,
green inchworm falling in.
Birches drip,
maples bud,
yellowthroats sing
"witchety-witchety" around the pond.
Frogs splash in rising reeds.
May springs for snow,
sponges rain,
Otter Creek spates to Lake Champlain.

We wriggle from the wet
like worms who've found the sun,
sprout images from upside down.

— *Charlotte, Vermont, May 29, 2017*

Santa Fe Yoga

We yogis arrive with stone shards rattling in our joints:
steel tendons, squeaky hips, spongy disks bracing brittle backs.
We spread our legs, plant our heels,
breathe like camels sailing the Sahara,
like ancient warriors pushing chariots up the mountain
lunging East from West.
We'll return to a living world from Shivazana's peaceful pose,
Namaste hands clasped before our hearts
like butterflies come to feed at salty puddles.

Rachel directs us to cat-cow,
down-dogging, spreading hands, tucking toes,
bending knees, shin to ankle bones,
heads pointing to the sky,
inhaling Mother Earth.

We stand and roll each foot over a yellow tennis ball,
push back heels, break down fascia
that sheathes our muscles,
flows like cheesecloth
within our caterpillar carapace.

I wonder what fellow practitioners think,
tucked into sweat suits, shorts, spaghetti straps,
breathing deeply like zinnias and sunflowers
absorbing summer sun.
I wish we could talk amongst ourselves
when we put away our sticky mats,
drop our eyes to seal yoga's covenant with the self.
We stack wooden blocks on shelves,
coil, arrange blue-braided belts in a basket,
slip silently towards the door.

— *July, 2015*

Horsetail

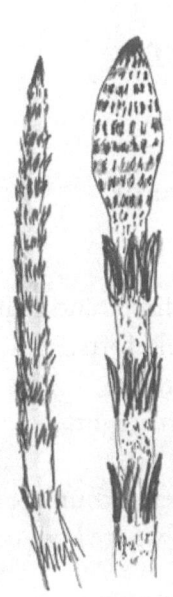

Hey little fella,
popsicle stick,
green umbrella,
poking fun at tulips,
tickling mallards
nesting in the ditch.

— *Skagit Valley, 2020*

People Power

I'm searching Pino Arroyo,
the grassy mesa where,
twenty years ago,
kids dragged sycamore limbs and branches
over desert sands to build forts,
dig out clay banks, make fire,
roast hot dogs, spend the night.

I'm stumbling on scattered chunks of wood,
a gully of tumbleweeds where boys once slept.
Outliers have vanished.
The ground is bare.

I wonder what boys learned,
propping up clubhouses, raising painted tribal flags,
the chasers and the chased.

I wonder what girls learned,
creating a village with tripods and tarps,
what they talked about when they settled in.

The kids grew up and graduated.
I don't know where they are or what they do.

I wonder about children everywhere.
Who will rule the world?

— *Albuquerque, New Mexico, 2019*

Pecos Raven

At Pecos pueblo,
warriors traded children,
buffalo hides for corn.
The church bell tower rings
for Olive Shell and Turquoise.

Mistletoe is ripe.
Townsend Solitaire serenades.
Pinacaté comes to pray.

Sentry raven hunches
over two red stones.
At noon,
wind ruffles.
She nods,
black angel on the wing.

— April, 2013

Notes:
Pecos Pueblo Spanish mission church. Pecos, New Mexico, 1717. Pecos
National Monument.

Round balls of mistletoe parasitize one-seed juniper.

Townsend's Solitaire, the only winter bird in northern New Mexico that
stakes out a territory. Feeds on mistletoe berries and spreads its seeds on
branches.

Pinacaté - A large black Southwestern beetle of the genus *Eleodes*. When
threatened, it tips its rear end up, points its head down, and remains still.
Common daytime wanderer on cold spring days.

3:01 AM

We lie in bed like fallen stars,
molten sand bubbling dreams,
Mom and Dad bobbing
in a wooden boat
flailing golf club fishing rods,
laughing with scotches
splashing from glass bowls.
Dad putts a white ball
across a green stretching into space.
I flinch with ocean lightning,
sharks jumping over the bathtub boat.
We four kids swim and talk with dolphins.
A breath of wind drops acorns through the ceiling.
We come about,
our spinnaker blown out,
first light tumbling through the sheets.

— *Santa Fe, New Mexico, November 26, 2013*

Bosquitos

My niece, Sarah Streng, created a children's nature group to explore the Rio Grande.

I meet the Bosquitos:
pints, quarts, gallons of curiosity,
bulging eyes, sniffing noses,
busy hands, fluffy fledglings
waddling between the cottonwoods.

Zen and Amadeus lead us
under Russian olive branches.
We duck through the willow thicket.

I teach the kids to whisper,
to use sign language when we see a bird,
one for white, two for blue,
three for black, four for robin red,
a wavy hand for flight,
index finger for a junco,
a pecking finger for a flicker,
a duck, a silent quack.

Amelia and Clementine gather sticks
to draw in mud: birds, crazy creatures.
Zen and Amadeus craft dinosaurs.

On an island, a patch of white gulls
tuck their heads under wings.
Others bow, spilling water off their caps.

A flock of snow geese fly above us.
A bald eagle would be rare.

What is silent song
when we pour ourselves into the river,
when we fill our jugs with melted snow?

— *Corrales, New Mexico, Winter, 2013*

Land of Shuar

Like the Shuar, we are children of the forest.

I cross the river
into the land of Shuar,
Jivaro legends dispelled,
shrunken heads of demons,
desiccated amidst the sultry din
of bulldozer civilization moving in.

If the jungle's trail is broken,
vines repair.
If land is cleared, people moan,
soils erode, jaguars rare.
To slash, to burn, to drill for oil,
to spill the future for present spoils.

At dawn, tinamous whistle,
antbirds wail.
Blue and Gold macaws scream for sun.
A puffbird snags an azure butterfly.
Flitting warblers, scorning cries,
woodnymph warnings,
corporate alibis.

I jump the stream,
push up a muddy switch-backed hill,
drum my feet between
walking palms, strangler figs.

The forest wreaks of rotting fruit,
sweet cinnamon, vanilla.
I bleed sweat.

Black conga ants devour a fleeting toad.
Limey leafcutter ants carve
pink corollas for their queen,
haul green confetti underground
to grow fungus to feed their larval throng.
Brigades of red army ants comb litter,
raze grasshoppers,
carry cockroaches in their jaws.
Saucer mushrooms, fuchsia caps,
smoky horns pop from rotting logs.
Cordyceps transform
a green katydid into a peachy crown.
Trees sprinkle amber trumpets, white lilies,
scarlet buttons, carillons of creamy butter palms.
A Woolly monkey,
a dozing sloth are fearful.
A Harpy Eagle may be near.

Drifting shapes and color phases,
plumed serpents, head-dresses,
spiraling palms, time and space delude.

On the lakeshore, blue-faced Hoatzins flop about the tangles.
Turquoise Swallow-tanagers snap up blue damsels.
Swallows fleece the tannic film of flies.

Between the sky and canopy,
hawk-eagles soar above the fray.

Eyes, ears, and nose can't fathom
all that sprouts, flowers, shares, depletes,
dies in kaleidoscopic form,
where the rotting anaconda tells us
we're living in some unfamiliar molecule
of unpatterned, changing life.

Time and space integrate in greens and golds,
reds and iridescence,
a loose organic lace,
some say the planet's frills,
others the jungle's gills.

— *Limoncocha, Ecuador, January, 1981*

Water

I flow from bone and brain
through arteries and veins,
appetite, heart.

I leach each breath,
prompt each drop,
relish run and riffle,
to feel the breeze like lily pad,
rush, rebound like dragonfly.

I swim to shed my skin,
to release me from sky and desert dust.

I wash in rain,
bath in snow.

I condense in lake,
shrink in stream,
funnel under cedar sweepers,
become the wave,
rise, fall,
swirl with current,
settle in the eddy.

I fish so water
will fill my gills,
cleanse what's left of me.

Ode to Poem

Beautiful is the poem
that speaks in curve,
rhymes in lace,
leaves you wet or dry;
reaps the sun,
chops the wind,
opens moon,
drops the snow;
rears its head
like a dancing mare
galloping in mud;
kisses a worm,
caresses the vole,
labors with jewels and crowns.

Each footprint begs a pool,
lines a cliff,
stanza salmon beat;
rod raised to cast, cut,
snake into the drum,
swim with sap,
snap the bud,
graft apricot to peach,
peel the apple,
punch with plum,
neither sour nor sweet.

Beware the poem that
sets fire to your heart,
leaves no water in the bucket.

Sponge poem from swamp,
drip with ancient rain.
Climb a tree.
One limb is all you need
to fell an image
soft and sweet.

Dig again to China.
You'll find a nail
or a nugget there
under your old fort.

Be a lightning bug or
Luna moth clinging to
your backdoor screen.

Prime your paint
with window washings,
bacon fat,
powdered bone
and blood.

Fly through the alley,
speak star to the star,
dot flag stripes:
red, blue, and green.

Jemez Apples

*Albuquerque's Menicucci family arrived from Lucca, Italy in the
early 20th century steeped in mushrooming tradition.*

In poetry, we share our secrets
like a phone call to a friend
about a fishing hole
tucked behind a barbed wire fence,
a solitary golden apple tree,
that I, like a nosey bear,
discovered when I hung a fishing fly
in an apple tree.

I revealed the tree to Mari whose son
Pat had sneaked me into family
Jemez mushroom haunts.
Mari confided that her dad would return
with porcini and apples.
Was it Papa who tossed the core?
Had he discovered a tree upstream
in a meadow lumber camp?

> In late August,
> you can cross the bridge,
> pass the monastery,
> a guardrail on the right.
> Search the river gulch below
> through scrawny elms,
> bluish junipers.
> No need to take fishing rod.
> Luck is what you'll need.

— *Jemez Springs, New Mexico, 2003*

Sandhill Cranes

A Blue Heron gazes over a gopher hole,
a busker stealth with silver sword.
A flock of Horned Larks swirl,
settle in with cows.

Cochineal-capped Sandhill Cranes,
draped in gossamer and challis,
pry alfalfa from frozen ground,
sew dairy must into angel wings.

At noon, a pair of cranes jig like kites,
joust like bobbing cobras,
dust devils dashing to the sky.

I breathe into their funnel.
We circle the fading moon.

— *Las Uvas Valley, New Mexico*

Pharaoh

Like ancient pharaohs,
should we have our way?
Giving, grabbing,
claiming odds in cardboard boxes,
leaving ends outside the door:
projects, chests and sets,
yearbooks, baby clothes,
bicycles, bassinettes,
fishing rods, picture frames,
a ball of twine,
a roll of tape, tarnished time.
Moving what for whom and why:
materialism, altruism,
needs and wants,
scythes and rakes,
33's and 45's,
Laurie's easel, a slew of paints.
We'll leave behind the red picnic table,
sell the ping-pong set,
an orange bumper jack that saved
my truck deep in mud in Mexico,
a rusted railroad jack
Chinese men cranked
to stake the West.
We'll save homemade brooms,
corn shellers, braces, bits,
pickle and jelly jars,
burlap sacks, my old guitar.
I'll dig pink *penstemons* I raised from seed.
We'll leave the swing for the buyer's kids,
but take the cider press.

— *Albuquerque, New Mexico, 2003*

Blueberries

To discourage robins,
we orchard people cover two rows
of blueberries with nylon netting,
create a long cage over rambling shrubs,
circle the bottom with chicken wire.

Ripening berries huddle
in their sunny tunnel:
sour June, sweet July.

I feel for fruit,
my fingers feed
like hatchling snakes.

I drop blueberries
into a yogurt cup
that hangs around my neck.

I dump loads in my cooler.
I imagine a peck of pies.

When I smell pancakes,
I have no mind for words.

— *Skagit Valley, Washington, 2019*

Gila Farm

Bonnie and Bonnet the goats thrive in the valley.
Plenty of elm twigs for two.

Raising two goats,
Duston and Gretchen thrive in the valley.
Plenty of milk for two.

— *Gila, New Mexico, 2015*

Fire and Music

I.
Thousands of feet above the Gila valley,
the Whitewater Baldy fire has singed the Mogollons.
Tears salt the graphite grit of baked Chihuahua pine,
soak the charcoal of Gambel's and silverleaf oak.
The mountain bared its back to flames.

II.
Monsoon rain ploughs through hydrophobic dust.
Slag gathers in rocky crevices and slot canyons.
Foam flushes through the talus on a raft of warbler bones,
ash of pink geraniums, sunken eyes of yellow columbine.
Black blood dumps the bilge through Gila's heart,
bloats the river with sticks, logs,
a goopy marinade that clogs fish gills,
coats the cobbles, kneads sand into greasy crud.
Chubs and suckers flounder on the banks.
Herons and vultures feast by day, raccoons by night.
What happens to soft-shelled turtles?
Have they dug deeply into summer sand?
What happens to loach minnow and spikedace?
Is the dirge too dense for little fish to tap a spring?

III.
Chocolate sediment settles
in a hole behind Duston's and Gretchen's hogan
set above the irrigation ditch: sculpted mud, rounded river rock;
flagstone pried out of Mule Mountain volcanic cribs
for her piano floor; belly walls to store wood heat
from elms and cottonwoods; thick earth to buffer June, July,
like thighs and butts of angus in the pasture;
oak limbs radiating from the ceiling hoop.

It's time to stucco.
Mud is free,
like the bear tooth Duston fit to fill a gap
to save a dentist bill.
They shovel loads of fire mud
into the wheelbarrow to fill cracks, to smooth the walls.
They load their hods, sweep their trowels across the parapet.

Duston naps after lunch, dreams of road-killed elk,
jujubes, popcorn, his pillow soft as a turkey's breast.
Gretchen feeds the goats.

IV.
I miss sitting outside the barn with Duston
watching Red-tailed Hawks;
falling silent when cranes purr overhead.

I'll return to Gila soon.
Spot will dodge a rattlesnake.
We'll enjoy Gretchen's red chile enchildadas,
melted goat cheese, onions fat and sliced,
crackers loaded up with succotash,
admire quarts of Super Sioux tomatoes,
piles of delicata squash.

V.
Gretchen composes
music from the lair of twining beans,
whispers of spinning windmill blades,
dust devils that whip the chicken coop.
I feel a fugue bumping on the river bed,
a sonata bubbling in the ditch.

— *Gila, New Mexico, 2012*

Enbom Lake

In November's emerald folds,
deep trout hold
like bottles on the bottom.
Blue sun warms my icy fingers.
The silver surface sucks
tight against my waders.
Sheathed in spongy neoprene,
I fin my boat through rotting weeds.

A mayfly sails across the lake
climbs aboard,
my fishing net its prow,
a wisp of wings too late
to find a mate.

The lake turns black with the falling sun.
A muskrat breaks from shore,
reverses course,
leads me home.

— *Jicarilla Apache Reservation*
Dulce, New Mexico, November 6, 1993

Plums

I wish I could pick ripe plums now.
It doesn't work that way.
You wait. You wait some more
if you want all they come to earth to share.

Sleep under the tree.
Pray to purple planets,
a plum falling to your touch.

— *Bellingham, Washington, September, 2021*

Hin-mah-too-yah-lat-kekht

"From where the sun now stands, I will fight no more forever."
In 1877 after escaping the U.S. cavalry in Yellowstone, Chief Joseph
and the Nez Perce surrendered after the Battle of Bear Paw near
Laurel, Montana.

Chief Joseph fights no more.
Our treaty broken like a beaver stick,
his spirit settled in Idaho,
his grave in Washington
on a hill where one tree grows.

Fleeing General Howard,
Joseph and his people punched through sagebrush,
shuffled horses' hoofprints
over Clark's Fork gravel bars,
skirted rapids,
forded runs.

I watch a junco peck through granitic scree
below a patch of fireweed.
Little bird flashes its white tail feathers,
dabbles with a Nez Perce bead.

— *Clark's Fork River, Wyoming, 2008*

Sidewalking

In elm and maple shade,
green moss framed each limestone sidewalk slab.
I traced my fingers over crinoid stems and fossil worms.

In spring and summer,
we kids drew chalk squares,
played hopscotch and Mother May I.

In fall, I raked leaves over raised edges
to pile up and burn.

On rainy days, I jumped puddles,
running fast to Ricky's house.

In winter, I skated icy patches to school.

Evenings, when the lamplighter climbed
his ladder, my father and I coursed
beside flat-topped privet hedges,
passing under sassafras and oaks,
kicking acorns and buckeyes
across the squares.
Dad warned me,
"Step on a crack,
break your mother's back."

I've wondered for years,
why not his back, or mine?
Why Mother's?

Even now,
I step over cracks
as if a boy might trip
on Dad's advice.

— *Glendale, Ohio, 1950's*

Harmony

My Aunt Daisy Fisher (1875–1970), lived in Hamilton, Ohio.
Victorian, idealist, social reformer who recited Shakespeare sonnets,
Robert Burns, and George Sims' "Ostler Joe" (1886).

Awake at dawn,
I notice a doe with two fawns curled up under the plum.
Peace, I think,
Aunt Daisy in her rocking chair reciting "Ostler Joe."

Her voice, my god so sweet,
a story so dark it seemed, until I listened again,
her remnant Scotch *a-gain*, and wondered why she'd share.
Did she fear my innocence, who I'd become?
Her voice melodious, full of love and despair,
telling this story of Joe, the hired stable hand,
his wayward wife who returns to him who loved her,
who comforts her in death.

Aunt Daisy had taken in troubled girls,
preached kindness to me *a-gain, a-gain*.
When she died, this stanza came to me:

> Lay down
> under the apple trees.
> Know the lion in the hills,
> the people you can trust.
> Use kind words to
> allay fear and lust.

Harvester Ants

Below the volcano,
on the basaltic outwash plain,
red ants radiate
along paths of pheromones,
a steady mission
to sort seeds from sand,
to feed larvae and their queen.

My jeans tucked into my socks,
I survey a mound for heishi.

Workers flow from their nest with empty chops,
return with snips of leaves and insect wings
like slaves of conscience,
carting wishes, storing dreams.

— *Albuquerque Volcanoes, New Mexico, September, 2006*

Note:
Heishi are shell beads made by ancestors of modern Pueblo people.

March Song

Robin, lead to your bed of worms.
Tickle me with your rosy feet.
Tilt your ear to mine.

With rain,
I've gathered myself from earth's well.
My gift returns yours, robin,
as you do, my soul,
to rinse your feathers with my words.

— *Santa Fe, New Mexico, 2014*

Bragging Rights

The Henry's Fork soothes the evening
like apple cider flowing to the Snake.
I've pulled up my waders, tied my boots,
stepped down the grassy bank to fish.
I meet a man casting black midge flies to rising trout,
trying out several rods lined up like shotguns
on the tailgate of his yellow, four-wheeled buggy.
He tells me he is searching for the rod
which best lays down
a fly like a dimple on a dime.

The fisherman splashes words on me
as if we were chatting at the kitchen sink,
as if fishing the Jordan,
cold water swaddling him after strokes and cancer.
He raves about his nephew playing
baseball for Idaho, "And can he hit!"
His daughter has a new baby.
His son "sets the world on fire"
selling ads for Google.

Downstream, a football field away,
a truck pounds the boards on the steel bridge.
"Galumph, galumph, rat-tat-tat."
A pair of silver cars roll into the starting gates,
rev their engines, "Vroom, vroom."

— *Chester, Idaho, 2014*

Espalier

Espalier sounds like French for breeze.
A hurricane might shake its trellis twigs,
spoon summer's luffing applesauce,
catch September bells when pears are ripe.

I recall *le boulangerie*, the bakery,
rolling Ohio vowels into my high school French,
a caterpillar lilt tangled in my own sweet whistle,
powdered sugar donut when I didn't know
a baguette was a hot dog-shaped loaf of bread.

I love willow baskets,
Goldsworthy's wrinkled rubs,
espalier, a wide-winged sculpture,
prima donna of Versailles,
braided fruitful hedge eye to eye with apricots.

I love weaving weeping willows into an urn,
strapping apical apple branches to ripple waves of fruit.

I love wood's wavy grains, bamboo hides,
lean-to's stacked against a rock.

I pinch and prune Akane apples and Bartlett pears.
I play with words.
I need to learn to trim poems to half their size.

Yet I'd hate to be strung up to steel wire ribbing,
trained to copper pipe.
I admit I'd grow more fruit
arm to arm, legs bowed like a jumping jack.

— *Bellingham, Washington, 2022*

I Want A Boat

if I wanted a boat, I would want a boat I could steer
— Mary Oliver

When I'm fishing,
I need a rowboat,
a dinghy that cuts through waves,
with a flat floor so I don't slip.

I admire the bow.
I feel its lead.
I trust the stern.

I like to settle on a lake,
dead-center on a bench,
or stand to ascertain
where swallows nip the surface
for mayflies, midges,
to notice dimpling trout,
to steer the boat into the sun,
troll close to shore or back away,
to search for color changes,
dark green to gold for weed beds,
drop-offs, thermoclines,
points that slope either way.

I guide the white lapstrake shell,
let it drift and swing with gusts
as if I'm cutting corners
through the woods.

I grip the oars to gather strength,
bend forward, pull,
then lean back churning blue and green,
water sheeting off each blade.

I love the rhythm of rowing repetition.
I could forget I've come to fish,
pause, let the boat rest
while I explore what lies below.

I drop anchor off a point as I would stake a claim,
to feel at home
where I've never been before.

Walden Pond and the Warming

To use a Boston phrase,
"Last winter was brutal."
Concord trains abandoned on the trestle.
City subways frozen to the tracks.

Barbara, who's known the pond for 80 years,
calls this winter too warm,
a pine needle path for fishermen
she saw cast silver spoons in January.
Bobbers bobbed.
Ice shacks never made it to the pond.

On the coldest days,
ice frittered with the sun,
slush collected,
oak leaves curdled in the coves.
Water beetles flushed,
a dusting of snow:
no sledding,
no snow days,
no snowplows,
split wood stayed stacked
against stone walls.
Locals wondered if
maples would run in March?
Do snow or ice matter
as long as the sap kettle fills?
Will Scarlet Tanagers be singing
from these treetops in fifty years?

Do caterpillars require
hard winters for cocoons?
Will winter warmth mean too many will survive
and strip the oaks?
Will Blue Jays disappear?
What would spring become
without the pink pouch of moccasin flower,
yellow pine pollen carpeting the shore,
pipsissewa nodding to nighttime fairies,
whisper of white-flowered Enchanter's nightshade,
the whistling Broad-winged Hawk?

Shall we romance rain as we did snow
when flakes buried nights,
when sun struggled to warm the shortest, bluest days?

— *Walden Pond, Massachusetts, 2012*

Note:
Barbara Davis lives on Concord Road across from Walden Pond.

Chimango

I catch you
posturing in a ponderosa pine
above the Chimehuin;
admire you whistling at campers
cleaning up their mess.

Perhaps a rainbow trout has washed
down from the Boca,
a *pancora* at the Junin bridge.

Tried the Hosteria?
Yesterday, green parakeets
screamed above the lawn,
a woman on her phone dropped a chunk of cheese.
After heavy rain, the garden reeks with worms.
Search the rotting stems of marigolds,
you'll find a grub.

Above the Fila Hua Hum,
I watch you strut, *Chimango,*
pause and scratch the pampas pasture
below the butts of white-faced cows;
you remind me of Cattle Tyrants
that ride the backs of bulls.

You could be flying
over the river's bluffs
searching Andean slopes,
peering down on wisps of fishermen,

then finish off their barbeque.
You recall my sparrow,
my hawk, all but the dove in me.

— *Junin de los Andes, March 13, 2006*

Notes:
Chimango Milvago chimango, an omnivorous raptor.

Boca del Chimehuin, mouth of *Lago Huechulafquen*, Argentina.

Pancora Pancora del Agua Dulce, an olive and orange freshwater crayfish.

Hosteria Hosteria Chimehuin, Junin de los Andes, Argentina.

Fila Hua Hum - Small, winding Patagonian river.

Cattle Tyrant *Machetornis rixosus* - yellow-gray robin-sized flycatcher.

Mulberry

Mulberry tree climbs
blue March skies to reach the sun,
spreads its emerald leaves,
explodes creamy clouds of pollen.

It swears patience
to courting finches, cooing doves.
If it could dance, it would shimmy-shake
for hummingbird figure-eights.
If silk-moths lived here,
we'd be weaving scarves and capes.

November's frost grips
stems and stipes.
With morning sun, they tremble, tumble,
flail and flop.
Green and yellow leaves
blanket gardens, patios, roofs.
like spilling beans, a quiet dump of snow.

It's death's drama:
leaves and limbs born to flap,
tear, tease, mend the wind,
endure the freezing rain,
gone to bones, breast to back.

Recall the Great-horned Owl
that calls out death in fall,
then hoots again at January mating time;
the unfeathered tree whose branches bend,
whips its twigs in winter,
stirs underground with life.

— *Bayita Lane, Albuquerque, New Mexico, 2001*

Showy Ladyslippers

I take my mother to haunts she's never seen,
the fern and horsetail realm;
pink pyrola nod beneath wispy tamarack.
White-flowered Enchanter's nightshade
draws us into sphagnum shade;
a forest for ladyslippers;
crab spider partners drool on rosy orchid bibs;
orchids tip white caps to wood frogs and rusty centipedes.

Mother dons her garden clothes,
blue skirt and blue boots as if joining a garden tour.
She wades behind me through peaty muck,
crossing rotting logs
without complaint
that mosquitoes are crazy for blue.

Stumbling on a patch of regal pink,
she will want to share
this spot with Mrs. Zimmerman,
who I know will want a clump of ladyslippers.
Mrs. Zim would insist on returning with a spade.
I love Mrs. Zimmerman,
but I brought her bass filets.

— *Walloon Lake, Michigan, 1995*

November Jay

A blue, spike-capped Stellar's Jay disappears
behind the ponderosa trunk.
She's quiet, hidden from my view.

She reappears:
flapping,
swooping,
gliding to a branch,
bobbing,
cackling.

Is she teasing?
Is she fearful or fascinated?

The trouble with birds is we don't speak their language.
The trouble with us is they don't speak ours.

— *Bellingham, Washington, November 3, 2019*

Barge Fishing

*While visiting Brazil's Pantanal with New Mexico teachers on a
natural history-cultural exchange trip.*

José leads me up the ropes.
We grab the towline,
leap onto the deck.
I rest on the railing
above deep gold current that wraps
the river bend.

We lope over rusted steel,
rotted planks,
peek into empty holds of the old rice barge,
duck under spider silk,
slap mosquitos that buzz for blood.

A yellow-breasted flycatcher
sallies from the bridge,
snags a big black beetle.
Crook-necked egrets,
like white-tied Brazilian buskers,
cruise by on hyacinth islets
ripped loose from the Pantanal.

We join other fishermen,
dressed in dungarees and colored shirts;
they stand on rounded rails,
cast beer-can coiled line,
chicken gizzards skewered on heavy hooks,
lead-weighted, dropping to muddy depths.

I'm the foreign fishing guy who
shoots a flashy silver lure
between rafts of diving cormorants.
White, sharp-billed terns dip for little fish.
We drink beer, chat, fiddle with our reels.

The sun squints behind the bridge.
José nods towards town.
We retrieve our lures,
say nothing to the men.
Off board, we dodge a preacher
blaring through a megaphone,
 "Venha para Jesus."
We move towards the plaza
sucked into country swing:
accordian, *zabumba*, guitar,
forró whirling dancers.
We mix with friends,
never see each other again.

— *Corumbá, Brazil, July, 2005*

Notes:
"Venha para Jesus", Come to Jesus

Zabumba, bass drum

Forró, Rhythmic Brazilian country polka

Bird to Be

My wife asks me
which creature I'd like to be.
I would be a bird for sure,
harrier or eagle,
not goat or flea.

A bird for sure,
not possum or raccoon,
snow leopard or elephant,
dung beetle, or baboon.

Which bird?
Not ostrich or kiwi,
rhea, or flightless grebe.
How about parrot poet,
or poet parrot,
surely one that flies,
not a penguin
in Antarctica where I'd surely die?

I'll wrap myself in gannet,
glide above the cliffs,
plunge for fish,
or become a peregrine
that stoops on desert doves
and ducks.

Try Golden Eagle,
a scouring Red-tailed Hawk.
I'd play with clouds,
dodge thunderheads.

A Snowy Owl in winter,
squinting on a haystack,
relieved of arctic hunger,
cries of polar bears.

A hummingbird,
too swift to catch my breath,
or let me see the world
the way I want,
more than pores or pollen,
a patient bird to spread the word.

Maybe a lark of sorts,
that sings up high,
drab browns with streaks,
glides down from sky.

A robin, ear to grass,
pipit scouring river stones,
bluebird plucking mistletoe?

Like starlings in purple robes,
I have more to do than dig for worms,
more to do than crows.

Why not be a bowerbird
weaving twigs, shells,
feathers, blue bottlecaps and ribbons
to frame an arc for earth?

La Señora of Pension Imperial

Below our white wood balcony,
I peek down on *La Señora*
made up with carmine lipstick,
white-powder on her nose.
Her black cloche blocks the sun.
I watch her toss breadcrumbs to a dove,
baby talk her cats, whisper to her dog.

La Señora runs Pension Imperial,
its courtyard rife with rusty floral iron,
blood red poinsettias in purple pots,
mauve bougainvilla, rosy mandevilla
that twines around a water fountain.

La Señora shuffles in white high heels,
sweeps papaya skins, banana peels,
waters pink geraniums, scrubs turquoise tubs,
soaks pillow cases in the laundry sink,
pins up sheets to dry.

She bows to a Jesus shrine,
her savior wreathed in neon plastic roses,
blessed with creamy callas.

La Señora climbs the stairs,
shakes her finger at me,
"No cocinando en los cuartos."

I nod, no cooking in the rooms.

She turns and mutters
to a hummingbird that
sips on pink impatience.

La Señora pauses on the railing,
which like our cerulean cloth ceiling,
hangs from some imaginary nail.

— *Latacunga, Ecuador, 1981*

Corydalis

I'm leaning into an Arizona sycamore near a
Gila River irrigation ditch when I spot a clump of
Corydalis aurea pushing up through fire silt.

Suck me down your golden chute.
Peel my eyes, pinch my ears,
squeeze my bleeding heart.
Let me roar with river's breath,
shoo me through the willows,
whistle with the red bird,
yelp with Gambel's Quail,
rise up when Black Hawk cries.

— *Ft. West Ditch, Gila River, March 16, 2013*
Gila, New Mexico

Note:
First spring after the Whitewater Baldy Fire.

Snails

I lie flat on the dock,
stare through
Walloon's water window
at the bottom of the lake.

A snail's furrow,
a swirling finger of
figure eights, grooves in marl.

A black-spiraled stupa
rides bareback on a clam.
I wait for the snail to wobble,
as if patience will turn a stone.

— *Walloon Lake, Michigan, 2006*

Sweet Peas

Pink and white sweet peas
ramble towards the sky;
sweet peas lush as gods and goddesses
regale kingdoms, queendoms,
scent the heavens with telltale bliss.

I play court jester,
ensure gardeners get our share.
I slice off stems below curling tendrils,
wide-winged branches, wayward shoots
that flop on spinach and Swiss chard.

At the kitchen sink, I poke hooded stems
into a brass frog at the bottom of a vase.
They nudge and roll off each other like pick-up sticks,
top heavy as lollipops.

If sweet pea bonnets could flip their flaps,
they'd surely fly away.

— *Bellingham, Washington, 2023*

Naked

Give in, my friend,
to nakedness,
our beastly burden packed
into our crocodile;
we who run with antelope,
swing with lemurs,
hang with sloths,
delicate as ptarmigan
who vanish in the snow.

Goose Eggs

When the Canada goose pops up,
I'm searching shallow water,
turning river rocks for bugs.

With a whip-like neck,
black-capped, pied cheek patch,
she rises from the grass,
waddles to the river's edge,
drops her beige belly,
paddles across the current to her gander.

I creep up the islet,
part a shock of red willows,
lean over a basket-full of cream-colored eggs.

I've learned from barnyard geese
I might be trapped in the gander's sights.
He might chase me down the river.
Head held high, he puffs his chest
waiting for his mate.

I scramble to the near bank,
pretend as I did when I peeked
at presents as a kid.

— *Rio Grande near Pilar, New Mexico, 2008*

Dan and the Orb Weaver

In May, I was shaken by a rustling
in a field of Connelly Creek canary grass.
Could it be a bear waking from a nap?

I spotted Dan, a man new to me,
sitting on his haunches, cutting grass stems,
cocktail straws to sell, with his pocket knife.

We talked about plants, gardens,
a patch of watercress tucked behind blackberries.
He offered to take me to the spring.

In June, Dan, in blue jeans, tattered, checkered shirt,
a smile on his white-whiskered, sunburned face,
appeared on the porch of the red cottage above our garden.

He rolled his bandaged left hand in his leathered right.
I asked, "What happened, Dan?"

His pinky finger's gone, an errant saw, three weeks in bed.
He'd come to sleep behind the gazebo
under blue boughs of Norway spruce.

Dan diverted my attention to an orange spider,
an orb weaver who had staged her silk
along a steel railing leading to the house.
"She is beautiful. Oh my!"

Dan became a gardener here; he dug out wild buttercup,
laid in rows of basil, which became a thicket with summer heat.

After a first trimming during Covid,
Lovitt restaurant folded.
Dan vanished, no more straws or basil.

In September, the orb weaver bulges like an acorn.
I imagine Dan's headed to the firs and hemlocks
to gather chanterelles.
Will he chance upon an orb weaver,
a red-legged frog, a patch of aging nettles?
I wish I could tag along.

— *Bellingham, Washington, 2020*

Apples

I'm looking for a rainbow trout.
I saw one last fall,
but this afternoon,
I discover bobbing apples.

I wonder what happened to our local bear,
children who have never picked a peach or pear,
Santa Feans who pay good money
for windfalls at the farmer's market,
folks who will never know
a basket of fresh fruit, an apple tree,
those who do and haven't bothered.

In November, arctic weather shrinks the city.
Cedar smoke snakes
through naked box elders,
climbs through cottonwoods.
Limbs hover above a creek
no wider than a goose's wings.

I squat along the sluggish current
sorting through round and rotting apples
pinned amongst the cobbles,
squirreled between gobs of sticks and leaves;
red delicious soaking in backwash
under a swoop of limbs,
a robin's shaggy cup,
a magpie's twiggy oven nest.

I pile apples on the grass
flat from August
where a sow and cub bedded down.
I roll an apple in my hand.
A green caddis larva burrows
in its rotting flesh.
Mayfly wigglers, black pinhead midges
colonize its rubbery skin.

I wind upstream looking for apple trees
rooted in fallow pastures.
I duck under box elder arms and legs,
push through white prairie clover,
willow spindles that shroud a sunken pickup truck.

I find a shrouded tree with shriveled fruit.
Its golden apples have dropped for mice,
others chewed by deer.

I take a stick and swat the sagging branches
for hail-scarred apples, soft and sweet.
I stuff my pockets.
I fill my hat.

— *Santa Fe River, New Mexico, 2015*

Blacktail Bucks

Lying on sticks of shadows,
two velvet-antlered bucks
huddle under apple trees,
docile as a mound of hay,
pitchforks upside down.

The black-tails push off their haunches,
nibble clover, wander towards the street.

I wonder why they leave.
Maybe yellowjackets have arrived
to claim the fruit.
Have the deer had enough?

I often wonder what animals are thinking
when food is plentiful.
Do bucks or doe follow what their mother taught them,
where to go and when?

Thinking:

> Let's wander to the forest,
> nip at ninebark,
> idle under hemlock boughs,
> follow the fading fog.

— Bellingham, Washington, September, 2017